free indeed

DEVOTIONS FOR LENT 2017

AUGSBURG FORTRESS

Minneapolis

FREE INDEED
Devotions for Lent 2017

Writers: Anne Edison-Albright (March 1–11), Rozella Haydée White (March 12–18), Javier (Jay) Alanís (March 19–28), Philip Ruge-Jones (March 29–April 4), Jennifer Baker-Trinity (April 5–15)
Editors: Suzanne Burke, Laurie J. Hanson
Cover image: Rafael López
Cover design: Laurie Ingram
Interior design: Eileen Engebretson

ISBN 978-1-5064-1600-7

17 16   1 2 3 4 5 6 7 8 9 10

Welcome

Martin Luther wrote his Small Catechism for the home, so that parents could explain the most important things in the Christian faith to their children. He prepared brief explanations of the Ten Commandments, the Apostles' Creed, the Lord's Prayer, and the sacraments of baptism and communion, which were gathered together with other material related to Christian practices in the home and published in 1529. These basic questions and answers about the Christian faith continue to inspire and guide individuals and the church almost 500 years later.

Free Indeed brings Luther's Small Catechism into your home or devotional time during this year of observing 500 years of reformation. Each day features a reading from the catechism, accompanied by an evocative image, a quotation to ponder, a reflection, and a prayer. The writers bring their unique voices and wisdom to reflect on Luther's teachings on the basics of Christian faith and practice.

May this Lenten journey through Luther's Small Catechism strengthen your faith as you move toward the Easter feast. Because Jesus' life, death, and resurrection set us free to love and serve our neighbor, we are free indeed!

—The editors

March 1 / Ash Wednesday

The First Commandment

You shall have no other gods.
What is this? or What does this mean?
We are to fear, love, and trust God above all things.

To ponder

"O God—please give him back! I shall keep asking You."
—John Irving, *A Prayer for Owen Meany*

God is God

John's best friend, Owen, dies, and over the course of many years
John's prayer stays the same: give him back! There are people I

love as much as John loves Owen Meany, people I pray could come back from death. And people I desperately do not want to die.

A pastor once told a group to write down the thing we most feared losing. We did. "That's your god," he said. I looked down at the name of my idol and felt helpless. I knew I would continue to be afraid. But I also knew: no human being can or should bear the burden of being a god. It's not fair. No one can carry that weight. Furthermore, Jesus already has.

I'm still like John, praying for Owen Meany to come back. I'm still afraid of losing the people I love. I'm still sad when loved ones die and I wish they could still be with me, here. I'm also grateful that God is God, and I am not. That God is God, and my husband and children are not. We can keep praying, we can keep asking, as John does, because God is God, and God is love.

Prayer

God, you are God. You are love, and you are trustworthy. Thank you for being able to carry the weight of all of creation's hopes, dreams, fears, sorrows, and most heartfelt prayers. Be with us when we are afraid of losing what we love. Make all of our relationships as healthy as they can be. We will keep praying; we will keep asking you. In Jesus' name. Amen.

March 2

The Second Commandment

You shall not make wrongful use of the name of the Lord
your God.

What is this? or What does this mean?

We are to fear and love God, so that we do not curse, swear,
practice magic, lie, or deceive using God's name, but instead use
that very name in every time of need to call on, pray to, praise,
and give thanks to God.

To ponder

The collapse of the World Trade Center brought me to my
knees. I prayed, like so many Muslims . . . that one of us wasn't
responsible for that heart-stopping catastrophe. Twenty mis-
guided men became fused with more than a billion others in

6

the heat of a single conflagration, and we were left to eat the soot of their sins. That's the problem with tasking any one of us to represent all of us. —Beenish Ahmed, "Learning—and Unlearning—to Be an Ambassador for Islam"

In God's name

A group of clergy sat around a table debating whether it was necessary for Muslim leaders to apologize for or denounce a recent terrorist attack. One pastor said, "I'm not expected to defend Christianity every time a Christian does something terrible or violent in the name of God." "Aren't you?" said another. "I get asked to do that more and more." The pastors wondered if mainstream voices of love would get more air time than voices of extremism, fear-mongering, and hate.

Eventually, a rabbi, who had been listening quietly, cleared his throat. "I might have something to add to this," he said, "being a religious minority in America. And part of a group that has some experience with anti-defamation work."

The consequences when God's name is used wrongfully are real. For religious groups who are the targets of that violence, it is a matter of life and death.

Prayer

Gracious God, we call on your name in love, in hope, in thanksgiving, in supplication. When your name is used to promote hatred, use us to enact love. Amen.

March 3

The Third Commandment

Remember the sabbath day, and keep it holy.

What is this? or What does this mean?

We are to fear and love God, so that we do not despise preaching or God's word, but instead keep that word holy and gladly hear and learn it.

To ponder

The reverend of the church stopped her pleasantly as she stepped into the vestibule. Did he say, as they thought he did, "Auntie, you know this is not your church?" As if one could choose the wrong one. But no one remembers, for they never spoke of it afterward.

—Alice Walker, "The Welcome Table"

God's big welcome table

Church signs proclaim "All are welcome!" Church people worry about declining worship attendance and blame soccer. They worry about people with no church affiliation—and about people who say they are done with church. How will we attract young people? How will we attract people of color? How will we make the sabbath day a priority for our members again?

Alice Walker tells the story of an old, dying black woman who is literally thrown—picked up and thrown—out of a white church on a Sunday morning. Tossed out on the street, she meets Jesus. She walks with Jesus along the highway, ecstatic, filled with joy even in her moment of death. Jesus welcomes her.

It is one thing to say, "All are welcome." It is another thing to take an honest look around our holy spaces and see who has been excluded, and how, and why. A holy sabbath, a kept sabbath, is a welcome table.

Prayer

God, your welcome table has room for everyone and then some. Keep us honest, make us faithful, give us ears to hear and eyes to see beyond our own needs, wants, and stories. In Jesus' name. Amen.

The Fourth Commandment

Honor your father and your mother.

What is this? or What does this mean?

We are to fear and love God, so that we neither despise nor anger our parents and others in authority, but instead honor, serve, obey, love, and respect them.

To ponder

Stony the road we trod, bitter the chast'ning rod,
felt in the days when hope unborn had died;
yet with a steady beat, have not our weary feet
come to the place for which our parents sighed?
—James Weldon Johnson, "Lift Every Voice and Sing"

Listen

On Twitter, a beautiful sight: "You might be Lutheran if . . . you serve champurrado and pozole at your posada." Yes! This is a way many Lutherans honor the traditions of father and mother, grandmother and grandfather. I can appreciate this and honor my father and mother—one who has fond memories of Christmas Eve midnight mass in Latin, and one who grew up eating lutefisk for Thanksgiving dinner. If all of our parents sat around a huge table and shared childhood stories . . . it would take a long time. But we would listen, both to honor our elders and to be amazed by the diversity at the table and the unexpected ways God weaves our family stories together.

Listen! Lutheran voices are singing "Lift Every Voice and Sing." It honors the experiences of their African American parents, grandparents, and great-grandparents. I want to listen to that song. By listening well, I can honor my father and mother, and your father and mother too.

Prayer

God our parent, teach us to be good listeners. As you lovingly listen to us, may we listen to each other. Bless us with wise elders, leaders, and mentors in faith. In Jesus' name we pray. Amen.

The Fifth Commandment

You shall not murder.

What is this? or What does this mean?

We are to fear and love God, so that we neither endanger nor harm the lives of our neighbors, but instead help and support them in all of life's needs.

To ponder

A family operates differently when in the midst of a crisis. It may be hard to act lovingly and have good communication when a child is engaging in a behavior that irritates, worries, frightens, or harms other family members. However, even in the midst of living with special needs, healthy relationships can flourish when

intention is present to foster those relationships.
—Lorna Bradley, *Special Needs Parenting*

Help and support

"I love Luther's explanation of the fifth commandment. It's so broad! It's great."

"What's so great about it?"

"Well, everyone thinks it's the easy one, right? 'No murder.' Check! But Luther expands it to include anything we might do that would endanger or harm someone's life. No one gets through life without doing that."

I was about to go on and explain that even this law exists to remind us of our need for God's grace—when I remembered that I was talking to a combat veteran, a man who struggled with his role and actions as a soldier, a person who never once thought that the fifth commandment was easy.

"In fact," I said, "I think I may have broken the fifth commandment just now."

He shook his head. "No harm done," he said.

Prayer

God, we give thanks for your grace in a world where harm is real, and where sometimes we are the ones who harm others. Fill us with your love so that our relationships with others and with you might be healthy and loving. Amen.

The Sixth Commandment
You shall not commit adultery.
What is this? or What does this mean?
We are to fear and love God, so that we lead pure and decent lives in word and deed, and each of us loves and honors his or her spouse.

To ponder
If words are free why can't I spare the best for you?
—Julia Fordham, "Porcelain"

Love means being loving

Person A: If we were able to spend more time together,
                     I would feel happy.

Person B: What I hear you saying is, if we were able to spend
                     more time together, you would feel happy.

Pastor: That's great! You've been practicing! How did it feel?

Person A: Completely unnatural.

Person B: Like a robot.

Person A: Does anyone ever actually talk like this?

Pastor: Not very often. But that's the point. The way we
                     naturally talk to our spouses when we're angry is
                     no good. We get mean. We get contemptuous. And
                     contempt . . .

Person B: . . . is a marriage-killer. We've been paying attention.

Pastor: Good. Keep practicing the "I" statements and
                     reflecting back what the other person says. It might
                     feel more natural with time. Or not. The point is,
                     your spouse is worth the effort. It's not always easy
                     to be loving to the people we love.

Prayer

In all relationships, God, may we reflect your love and fidelity. Work through our communities of faith to support and strengthen loving relationships. In Jesus' name. Amen.

March 7

The Seventh Commandment

You shall not steal.

What is this? or What does this mean?

We are to fear and love God, so that we neither take our neighbors' money or property nor acquire them by using shoddy merchandise or crooked deals, but instead help them to improve and protect their property and income.

To ponder

For my careening cabbie, the infrequent and oft-exaggerated dangers of public life were clearly outweighed by the benefits of interacting daily with strangers. He welcomed their company not merely because they helped him make a living—they helped him feel alive. As he practiced hospitality toward the stranger, he grew more at home, embracing rather than fearing the tensions of diversity as a path of learning and living.

—Parker J. Palmer, *Healing the Heart of Democracy*

Bridging the distance between us

All of the first-year divinity school students stood in a single line across the middle of a long, narrow room. We were a diverse group: racially and ethnically, men and women, a wide age range, a lengthy list of Christian denominations, as well as atheists and agnostics. We stood in our line, and leaders asked us questions. It was going well. And then:

"Take a step off the line if you've ever stolen something."

Almost everyone took a step. I didn't. One of my classmates noticed and yelled, "Liar! Is the next question about lying, because this one needs to take a step for that!" Well, if they'd asked for people to take a step if they'd ever lied, I *would* have been in that group. But I wasn't lying about not stealing.

I've never stolen anything, but I participate in a culture where fear of stealing leads many of us to build higher and higher walls, to fear our neighbors and barricade ourselves in our castles.

The space between my classmate and me was wider than a step, and we knew it.

Prayer

God, tear down the walls of fear we build around us. Jesus, bridge our divides. Amen.

March 8

The Eighth Commandment

You shall not bear false witness against your neighbor.
What is this? or What does this mean?
We are to fear and love God, so that we do not tell lies about our neighbors, betray or slander them, or destroy their reputations. Instead we are to come to their defense, speak well of them, and interpret everything they do in the best possible light.

To ponder

We do not like her very much. We do not think she has a rich inner life or that God likes her or can even stand her. (Although when I mentioned this to my priest friend Tom, he said you can

safely assume you've created God in your own image when it turns out that God hates all the same people you do.)
—Anne Lamott, *Bird by Bird*

Generosity of spirit

"We call it 'generosity of spirit,'" said the corps member advisor. Her job was to train a room full of recent college graduates to be teachers . . . in five weeks. "You're going to need it. Basically, it means giving people the benefit of the doubt. Have high and consistent expectations for your students, but have compassion too. If you clash with your colleagues or your administrators, try to see it from their point of view. Choose to receive everyone and everything that happens to you in the best possible light."

One of the corps members raised his hand. He asked, "Will people be that generous with us?" She laughed. "What do you think I'm doing right now?" We laughed. "Seriously, though . . . yes. Every day. You won't believe the grace you'll get. You won't believe the grace you're going to need."

Prayer

Generous Spirit, compassionate God, thank you for the grace you freely give, the grace we so deeply need. May we freely and joyfully share and receive that grace. Give us generous spirits. Amen.

The Ninth Commandment

You shall not covet your neighbor's house.
What is this? or What does this mean?
We are to fear and love God, so that we do not try to trick our
neighbors out of their inheritance or property or try to get it for
ourselves by claiming to have a legal right to it and the like, but
instead be of help and service to them in keeping what is theirs.

To ponder

"Isn't it amazing that we keep on going? That we keep on
shopping for clothes and getting hungry and laughing at jokes
on TV? When our oldest is dead and gone and we'll never see

him again and our life's in ruins! We've had such extraordinary troubles," she said, "and somehow they've turned us ordinary."
—Anne Tyler, "People Who Don't Know the Answers"

Neighborliness

There's a popular meme on social media: "Don't compare your inside to someone else's outside." It's fitting, because social media is a likely place for those comparisons to happen, but it's also not a new thing. When we covet our neighbor's house, we imagine their house is in good order. We picture it as cleaner, more put together, and happier than our own.

The truth is that our troubles, even the extraordinary ones, are pretty ordinary. In every house you will find some longing, some yearning for life to be different. You will find people grieving, amazed that regular life can even continue.

Do we dare to go to our neighbors' homes and ask them how we can help? Is there joy we can share that will make all households happier?

Prayer

God, when my house is full of sadness, send me neighbors who can help. Send me as a neighbor to help others in need. In Jesus' name. Amen.

The Tenth Commandment

You shall not covet your neighbor's wife, or male or female slave, or ox, or donkey, or anything that belongs to your neighbor. *What is this? or What does this mean?*

We are to fear and love God, so that we do not entice, force, or steal away from our neighbors their spouses, household workers, or livestock, but instead urge them to stay and fulfill their responsibilities to our neighbors.

To ponder

The Wife: I am yours to do with as you will, Peter Semyonych.... If you want me, open your arms now and I will come to you.... If you love me, turn your back and I will leave,

and never see or speak to you again. . . . I await your decision.
—Neil Simon, "The Seduction"

Real love

I played The Wife. I was a freshman in high school, and Joe, a
senior, played The Seducer, Peter. I kind of coveted Joe, to be
honest. He was beautiful. Every night, at the end of our scene,
I got to put my hand on his chest and say, "No." And then I'd
launch into the table-turning monologue, where the wife re-
forms the seducer by giving him a choice.

The scene has stayed with me and has taken on new meaning
with time. In the scene, Peter is both sincerely romantic and
undeniably sinister. He is a serial adulterer who claims to love
the women he seduces. The wife, unnamed, changes everything
by naming this truth: coveting someone and loving someone are
two very different things. To covet a person is to objectify them.
To love a person is to realize they are a real human being. Not an
object. Not a prize. Real. When women become real to Peter, he
finds he can no longer treat them as objects to be won. He can't
be The Seducer anymore.

By the end of the play, I'd come to love my friend Joe. I didn't
covet him anymore: he was real to me.

Prayer

God, thank you for making us real and free. Use us to work
against all coveting and objectification of your creation. In Jesus'
name. Amen.

March 11

What then does God say about all these commandments?

God says the following: "I, the Lord your God, am a jealous God, punishing children for the iniquity of parents, to the third and the fourth generation of those who reject me, but showing steadfast love to the thousandth generation of those who love me and keep my commandments."

What is this? or What does this mean?

God threatens to punish all who break these commandments. Therefore we are to fear his wrath and not disobey these commandments. However, God promises grace and every good thing to all those who keep these commandments. Therefore we also are to love and trust him and gladly act according to his commands.

To ponder

"But *now*," says the Once-ler, . . .
"UNLESS someone like you
cares a whole awful lot,
nothing is going to get better.
It's not."
—Dr. Seuss, *The Lorax*

Love and the law

How do you react to the Once-ler's words? The way we respond to words of law and command can vary a lot from person to person, from situation to situation.

I used to have terrible insomnia and would lie in bed and replay every horrible thing I'd ever said or done. I called it my Movie of Shame. I told a colleague about it, and she said, "Well, that's pretty arrogant of you. If you're going to insist on hanging on to your guilt, what on earth do you need Jesus for?"

I was reminded of God's trustworthy love; I was made glad. Over time, the movie stopped. With a no-nonsense word of law, my colleague had shown me the gospel. God doesn't give us law to torment us. God gives us law because God loves us and wants us to live with each other and God in healthy, loving ways.

Prayer

Loving God, when we are weighed down by guilt and shame, free us. Forgive us, teach us to forgive, and teach us to live in healthy, life-giving ways. Amen.

The Creed: The First Article

I believe in God, the Father almighty, creator of heaven and earth.

What is this? or What does this mean?

I believe that God has created me together with all that exists. God has given me and still preserves my body and soul: eyes, ears, and all limbs and senses; reason and all mental faculties.

To ponder

I have come to believe that caring for myself is not self-indulgent. Caring for myself is an act of survival.

—Audre Lorde, *A Burst of Light*

Created in God's image

Believing that God created all makes a difference in how we interact with each other and with creation. We begin to see that everything and everyone is sacred, reflecting the beauty, depth, and breadth of God. Sometimes this reality is easier for me to grasp than another one—that I too am not only created by God but actually created in God's image. This truth can be daunting because I struggle with my own worth and enoughness. To believe that a bit of the divine resides in me means that the totality of my existence has the capacity to reflect the love, compassion, and humility that define the very character of God.

I'm learning that embracing the truth that God has created all and flows through all—including me—requires that I surrender to the fact that I am worthy and enough. It invites me to care for all aspects of myself in ways that honor the person who God created. It's not a selfish act to take time for myself. Rather, it's a practice of believing that the fullness of who I am requires attention so I may be of service to the world.

Prayer

Creator God, I believe in my head that I am created in your image, but my heart struggles to embrace this truth. Help my unbelief. Amen.

The First Article

What does this mean? (continued)

In addition, God daily and abundantly provides shoes and clothing, food and drink, house and farm, spouse and children, fields, livestock, and all property—along with all the necessities and nourishment for this body and life. God protects me against all danger and shields and preserves me from all evil. And all this is done out of pure, fatherly, and divine goodness and mercy, without any merit or worthiness of mine at all! For all of this I owe it to God to thank and praise, serve and obey him. This is most certainly true.

To ponder

People think pleasing God is all God cares about. But any fool

living in the world can see it always trying to please us back.
—Alice Walker, *The Color Purple*

Paying attention

There's a connection between having open ears, eyes, and minds and having open hearts. To have an open heart means that one is empathetic to others, to situations, and to causes. To have an open heart means that one is open to vulnerability, which leads to compassion. I believe that the journey to opening my heart is a lifelong journey that works in tandem with other senses and with other experiences.

This reality is connected to who God is and how God shows up for each and every one of us. It's tempting to believe that God shows up only in the material form. We notice this when we talk about being blessed because of having something or because a tragedy passed us by. The reality is that God doesn't necessarily make things happen or not happen. God doesn't provide for some and leave others lacking. God creates all and gives us the power to truly see one another and provide for each other in ways that reflect God's abundance. To be heart-centered and to live a life that reflects God's desire for all of creation means paying attention and noticing how life is unfolding around us.

Prayer

Loving God, remove the blinders from my senses so that I experience you in all whom I encounter. Amen.

The Creed: The Second Article

I believe in Jesus Christ, God's only Son, our Lord, who was conceived by the Holy Spirit, born of the virgin Mary, suffered under Pontius Pilate, was crucified, died, and was buried; he descended to the dead [or "he descended into hell," another translation of this text in widespread use]. On the third day he rose again; he ascended into heaven, he is seated at the right hand of the Father, and he will come to judge the living and the dead.

To ponder

There is nothing so secular that it cannot be sacred, and that is one of the deepest messages of the Incarnation.
—Madeleine L'Engle, *Walking on Water*

Restoration

I am a person of Christian faith because of the incarnation. The thought that a divine God would choose to reside in human flesh and walk among us remains one of the greatest mysteries and central tenets of my faith.

In a world that divides things into sacred or secular, Christianity offers an alternative, one that has the power to bring about restoration. Our brokenness is responsible for Jesus' journey to the cross. But by choosing to become human, God showed us that we are worth restoring. By living a life that encompassed all the joy and pain that come with existence, Jesus submitted to humanity. This submission leads to the promise of integration and wholeness, that all may come to know the liberating power of God. After Jesus' death, God's power was at work, helping us to see that the story doesn't end with death. The point is a life of restoration, one that brings all things together for good. No one and nothing is outside of God's restorative power.

Prayer

Spirit of the living God, fall fresh on us so that we may come to know your liberating power, which leads us to integration and wholeness. Amen.

The Second Article

What is this? or What does this mean?

I believe that Jesus Christ, true God, begotten of the Father in eternity, and also a true human being, born of the virgin Mary, is my Lord. He has redeemed me, a lost and condemned human being. He has purchased and freed me from all sins, from death, and from the power of the devil, not with gold or silver but with his holy, precious blood and with his innocent suffering and death.

To ponder

The cross is a reminder of how humans have tried throughout history to destroy visions of righting relationships that

involve transformation of tradition and transformation of social relations and arrangements sanctioned by the status quo.
—Delores Williams, *Sisters in the Wilderness*

Our view of the cross

My lived experience as a Black woman of Christian faith informs the way I interpret the death of Jesus on the cross. Black women have long been on the receiving end of violence and have suffered in every aspect of their lived experience. This means I and others reevaluate Jesus' suffering and death on the cross, and seek to move people from an individual to a collective focus.

Glorifying the suffering of Christ and degrading the goodness of a person have led to the justification of redemptive suffering, the perpetuation of injustice, and a complacency that prevents people from addressing oppressive systems and structures. They have also made it easier for people to focus on their individual state rather than the communal reality.

What if we viewed the cross and the human condition through an alternative lens, one that uplifts the uniqueness of Jesus' suffering and seeks to eradicate injustice, oppression, and suffering?

Prayer

Mothering God, help us to let go of ways of being and thinking that limit our knowledge and our experience. Open us up to new ways of thinking and being. Amen.

March 16

The Second Article

What does this mean? (continued)

He has done all this in order that I may belong to him, live under him in his kingdom, and serve him in eternal righteousness, innocence, and blessedness, just as he is risen from the dead and lives and rules eternally. This is most certainly true.

To ponder

We love because it's the only true adventure.
—Nikki Giovanni, "Love: Is a Human Condition"

Created for relationship

"To whom do you belong?" This is a question I often ask young adults to help them think through their identity and the question of belonging. To belong to God and to be able to articulate this reality leads to a different way of showing up in the world. When we know that we were created for relationship by a relational God, we begin to understand the importance of interdependence. We move from thinking solely about ourselves to thinking about our neighbors and the decisions we make.

Relationships are meant to be reciprocal. Our relationship with God is no different. We respond to who God is and what God has done because we love God and understand that relationships require effort. We know that life is better when we are loved and when we love. We know that life is best experienced in community—in spaces where we can share our fears and joys and questions. We know that this life is meant to be lived in ways that build up the body of humanity.

Prayer

God of all creation, help us to live in ways that are connected and to seek out ways of living and loving that model your relational presence. Where there is separation or division, bring us closer. Help us see the ways we fit together in order to reflect your divine image. Amen.

The Creed: The Third Article

I believe in the Holy Spirit, the holy catholic church, the communion of saints, the forgiveness of sins, the resurrection of the body, and the life everlasting.

What is this? or What does this mean?

I believe that by my own understanding or strength I cannot believe in Jesus Christ my Lord or come to him, but instead the Holy Spirit has called me through the gospel, enlightened me with his gifts, made me holy and kept me in the true faith, just as he calls, gathers, enlightens, and makes holy the whole Christian church on earth and keeps it with Jesus Christ in the one common, true faith.

To ponder

I hope you will go out and let stories, that is life, happen to you
. . . water them with your blood and tears and your laughter till
they bloom, till you yourself burst into bloom.
—Clarissa Pinkola Estés, *Women Who Run with the Wolves*

Strategic storytelling

The best stories bring about feelings of wholeness and com-
pletion, provide examples of love in various forms, or feature
characters who overcome struggle. Stories bind us together and
help us to see life in a different way.

The Hebrew scriptures contain stories of how God related
to the Israelites. The gospel story tells how God relates to humanity through the person of Jesus Christ. Jesus was a strategic
storyteller—a person who knows how to use stories to convey
messages, evoke feelings, and compel people to act.

The Holy Spirit continues in this tradition, drawing out
stories within us and others that point to who God is and what
God desires. We are called to co-create with God stories of liber-
ation, freedom, compassion—and ultimately love. In doing this,
we become more fully ourselves and create life-giving relationships that transform all of creation.

Prayer

Holy Spirit, bring to life the stories you have implanted so that
we fully embrace who we are and whose we are in faith. Amen.

The Third Article

What does this mean? (continued)

Daily in this Christian church the Holy Spirit abundantly forgives all sins—mine and those of all believers. On the last day the Holy Spirit will raise me and all the dead and will give to me and all believers in Christ eternal life. This is most certainly true.

To ponder

Be faithful to the task of making justice and peace flourish; opt for God's cause and the law of love.

—Ada Maria Isasi-Diaz, "Mujeristas: A Name of Our Own!!"

Freed to work for justice and peace

The Holy Spirit is constantly nudging us to live into the forgiveness of our sins. We move from focusing on ourselves and never believing we have enough to being open to the world around us and believing God's promise of abundance. We act in ways that are freeing and seek out opportunities to serve and give and love. We are empowered to co-create and transform present-day realities. We are freed from sin to live in ways that promote justice and peace so that all may experience the love of God. This is not just a "hereafter hope." We pray that heaven on earth comes today, not tomorrow.

This way of thinking and being isn't possible without the Holy Spirit reminding us again and again of our purpose. Listen. Pay attention. Follow. The Spirit will lead you to a place where all flourish.

Prayer

God, you ask us to do justice, love kindness, and walk humbly with you. Help us to follow your Holy Spirit so that we may create your beloved kingdom here on earth. Amen.

The Lord's Prayer: Introduction

Our Father in heaven.

What is this? or What does this mean?

With these words God wants to attract us, so that we come to believe he is truly our Father and we are truly his children, in order that we may ask him boldly and with complete confidence, just as loving children ask their loving father.

To ponder

This is my Father's world;
I rest me in the thought
of rocks and trees, of skies and seas;
his hand the wonders wrought.
—Maltbie D. Babcock, "This Is My Father's World"

Deeply loved

The hymn "This Is My Father's World" praises God and reminds us that we are a part of the creation. God is the ruler of the universe, of sea and sky and of all the living creatures of the world. And yet God knows us personally and intimately and, as the hymn says, speaks to us everywhere.

We are deeply loved and cared for by God. Because of this, we can approach the Father in heaven as a small child who trusts her parents for every good thing, for food and clothing, and for special care when she is ill or troubled. Each of us can boldly ask God, who fashioned all of creation, for what we need.

Prayer

Just as Jesus called his daddy "Abba," so do I call you "Papa." Speak to me this day through the beauty of your creation. Amen.

The First Petition

Hallowed be your name.

What is this? or What does this mean?

It is true that God's name is holy in itself, but we ask in this prayer that it may also become holy in and among us.

How does this come about?

Whenever the word of God is taught clearly and purely and we, as God's children, also live holy lives according to it. To this end help us, dear Father in heaven! However, whoever teaches and lives otherwise than the word of God teaches, dishonors the name of God among us. Preserve us from this, heavenly Father!

To ponder

Holy, holy, holy, my heart, my heart adores you.
My heart is glad to say the words: You are holy, God.
Santo, santo, santo, mi corazón te adora.
Mi corazón te sabe decir: Santo eres Señor.
—Argentine traditional

Holy, holy, holy

This traditional Argentinian hymn reminds us of the holiness of our God. God's holiness does not mean that we cannot approach God, but that the one we know as the Ancient of Days is eternal and worthy of our deep respect and love. This song praises, honors, and blesses the name of the one we love. The words remind us that we are called to lead lives that reflect God's holiness and way of being in the world.

To be holy means we are set apart for works of mercy and justice in the world. Relating justly and honorably with all people is a value we cherish and teach. Anything less is to harm our neighbor who is created in the image and likeness of God. We pray that we might live faithful lives of service so that we may honor the name of the Holy One.

Prayer

Sanctify me, O Lord, for your service. Amen.

March 21

The Second Petition

Your kingdom come.

What is this? or What does this mean?

In fact, God's kingdom comes on its own without our prayer, but we ask in this prayer that it may also come to us.

How does this come about?

Whenever our heavenly Father gives us his Holy Spirit, so that through the Holy Spirit's grace we believe God's holy word and live godly lives here in time and hereafter in eternity.

To ponder

We believe in the Reign of God—the day of the Great Fiesta when all the colors of creation will form a harmonious rainbow,

when all peoples will join in joyful banquet, when all tongues of
the universe will sing the same song.
—Justo L. González, "A Hispanic Creed"

The day of the great fiesta

Justo González refers to the kingdom of God as a reign or rule
when all of the creation will be in harmony. In his popular creed
he invites us to believe that in this reign everyone is invited and
no one is left out. He shares Martin Luther's confidence that the
rule of God comes to us as a gift of grace and joy.

We see the signs of God's reign at our baptism when we
receive the Holy Spirit and the assurance that we belong to the
family of God. We see it when the church embraces us with hospitality and together we sing songs of praise that fill our hearts.
We see it when we confess our faith and promise to lead lives
of goodwill toward everyone. Because we seek to do the will of
God, we pray that the Holy Spirit will use our spiritual gifts and
talents to create a world where all people will have their needs
met and where everyone will share in the bounty of God's grace.
We pray that we may play a part in making this new creation a
fiesta for everyone to enjoy and celebrate the goodness of God!

Prayer

Come, Holy Spirit, and renew the whole creation! Amen.

The Third Petition

Your will be done on earth as in heaven.

What is this? or What does this mean?

In fact, God's good and gracious will comes about without our prayer, but we ask in this prayer that it may also come about in and among us.

To ponder

When we pray that God's will be done on earth as in heaven, we acknowledge our obedience to the divine authority. The acknowledging of the desire that God's will be done on earth where we are implies, by contrast, that our will is not the one to govern our lives on earth: *"Your will be done."* Jesus teaches us to pray acknowledging that God's will is to be supreme over our human will.

—Alicia Vargas, "The Prayer That Jesus Taught Us"

Trusting God's lead

Have you looked up to the heavens and wondered what the purpose of your life might be? You may have asked, why am I here? Before I became a pastor I practiced law in South Texas. I thought I had found my calling in life. It was a very fulfilling vocation. I often sensed that some folks were looking for someone they could talk to about their problems. I would pray with my clients and ask God to show them what they should do, what direction they should take. When my pastor started insisting that I go to seminary, I was a bit confused. On one occasion he introduced me to a church leader who wrote to inform me that he was praying for me. I started looking up to the heavens and asked for divine guidance.

After much prayer I decided that this must be the will of God and that God was asking me to trust that this was something I was called to do. As I learned to let go of the work that I so enjoyed and to trust that God was leading me in a new direction, my prayer became "Your will be done."

Prayer

Help me to listen to your Spirit and follow your will. Amen.

The Third Petition

How does this come about?

Whenever God breaks and hinders every evil scheme and will—as are present in the will of the devil, the world, and our flesh—that would not allow us to hallow God's name and would prevent the coming of his kingdom, and instead whenever God strengthens us and keeps us steadfast in his word and in faith until the end of our lives. This is God's gracious and good will.

To ponder

Inside of me there are two dogs. One is mean and evil and the other is good and they fight each other all the time. When asked which one wins I answer, the one I feed the most.

—Sitting Bull, in *Sitting Bull: The Collected Speeches*

Fight the good fight

In his attempt to reform the church of his day, Martin Luther made many enemies—people who did not agree with him and his interpretation of the scriptures. At times, Luther felt as if the whole world had turned against him. He believed that his fiercest enemies, however, were the devil, the world, and his own sinful nature. Luther's inner struggle was so intense that he once threw an inkwell at a wall in his room, as if throwing it at the devil.

Eventually Luther found consolation and assurance in the fact that he was a baptized child of God. God's grace had been poured out on him and would not let him go. Luther could confidently say, "I am baptized!"

Prayer

Lord, keep me faithful to your will for my life and the world. Amen.

The Fourth Petition

Give us today our daily bread.

What is this? or What does this mean?

In fact, God gives daily bread without our prayer, even to all evil people, but we ask in this prayer that God cause us to recognize what our daily bread is and to receive it with thanksgiving.

What then does "daily bread" mean?

Everything included in the necessities and nourishment for our bodies, such as food, drink, clothing, shoes, house, farm, fields, livestock, money, property, an upright spouse, upright children, upright members of the household, upright and faithful rulers, good government, good weather, peace, health, decency, honor, good friends, faithful neighbors, and the like.

To ponder

I hunger for filling in a world that is starved.
—Ann Voskamp, *One Thousand Gifts*

Compartir el pan

My father and mother had a store in South Texas when I was growing up. We sold a great deal of food to folks from both sides of the U.S.–Mexico border. When my parents taught me to treat everyone with respect, that was their way of telling me that everyone had dignity. At times we would give people at the store a *pilón*, or extra portion. That was our way of sharing and showing gratitude. My mother also would ask me to take plates of food from our kitchen stove to the neighbors or to someone in need. I have fond memories of those days when *compartir el pan* ("share the bread" in Spanish) meant that I would take a portion of the food from our table and share it with our neighbors.

South Texas was farm country, and often our farmer friends and ranchers would bring their produce to us as gifts of the harvest. We were connected to each other and to the land in a way that revealed the goodness of God for all of the creation. We were sustained by the land and the friendships that gave us life.

Prayer

Lord, grant me a hunger for just sharing that all may be filled. Amen.

The Fifth Petition

Forgive us our sins, as we forgive those who sin against us.
What is this? or What does this mean?
We ask in this prayer that our heavenly Father would not regard our sins nor deny these petitions on their account, for we are worthy of nothing for which we ask, nor have we earned it. Instead we ask that God would give us all things by grace, for we daily sin much and indeed deserve only punishment. So, on the other hand, we, too, truly want to forgive heartily and to do good gladly to those who sin against us.

To ponder

We know that in all creation only the human family has strayed. We know that we are the ones who are divided and we are the

ones who must come back together. Teach us love, compassion, honor that we may heal the earth and heal each other.
—Steven McFadden, *The Little Book of Native American Wisdom*

Healing for broken people and places

In the ancient Greek sport of archery, to miss the mark meant that the archer failed to hit a bull's-eye with his arrow. We "miss the mark" when we sin by being hurtful or dishonest in our dealings with others. We miss the mark by failing to see that we are all connected to God and to the creation.

Native Americans have long taught that we are all related and that what affects one affects all. As a result, they recognize that we have a responsibility to care for each other and the creation. In their prayers they ask for wisdom to heal the divisions between people and to heal the creation that has been spoiled by greed and misuse.

Our relationship with God, the source of all that is good, makes it possible for us to bring healing to a broken world. We do this as we receive forgiveness and forgive others. We do this as we care for each other and for the world that God loves.

Prayer

Lord, let my prayer bring healing and unity to others and the earth. Amen.

The Sixth Petition

Save us from the time of trial.

What is this? or What does this mean?

It is true that God tempts no one, but we ask in this prayer that God would preserve and keep us, so that the devil, the world, and our flesh may not deceive us or mislead us into false belief, despair, and other great and shameful sins, and that, although we may be attacked by them, we may finally prevail and gain the victory.

To ponder

Deny me those gratifying invitations, those highly interesting contacts, that participation in the brilliant movements of our age, which I so often, at such risk, desire.

—C. S. Lewis, *Reflections on the Psalms*

Prayerful resistance

Years ago I was a trial attorney. As a public defender I prosecuted folks whose actions had injured others. It was not an easy task. Many folks had unwittingly fallen into a trap of misguidance and misdirection. They failed to think seriously about the consequences their actions would have on others or themselves. They had been tempted by lies of quick and easy money or self-gratification. They had been entrapped by their own schemes and drawn deeper and deeper into illegal activity.

C. S. Lewis reminds us how easy it is for all of us to be misled by others, misdirected by our own self-centeredness, and deceived by temptations that appear to be innocent. In the Lord's Prayer we entrust ourselves to God's care and keeping, knowing that Christ has already defeated temptation and sin.

Prayer

Help me not to be deceived, O Lord, during times of trial. Amen.

The Seventh Petition

And deliver us from evil.

What is this? or What does this mean?

We ask in this prayer, as in a summary, that our Father in heaven may deliver us from all kinds of evil—affecting body or soul, property or reputation—and at last, when our final hour comes, may grant us a blessed end and take us by grace from this valley of tears to himself in heaven.

To ponder

I have a dream that one day on the red hills of Georgia, the sons of former slaves and the sons of former slave owners will be able to sit together at the table of brotherhood.

—Martin Luther King Jr., "I Have a Dream"

Sitting for justice

African American spirituals gave voice to the experience of being enslaved and longing for freedom. In a time when they were given no voice or power, people sang their woes in the heat of the cotton fields.

Years later, Dr. Martin Luther King Jr. dreamed of a new day and fought for civil rights. He joined forces with the seamstress Rosa Parks when she refused to surrender her seat on a bus. They believed that all men and women are created equal. From them we learn that we condone evil when we don't question injustice. There are times when we need to take a seat for justice and times when we need to take a stand and speak.

Today we continue to deal with the results of the evil institution of slavery. Its legacy of racism affects all of us. We ask for the courage and the wisdom to combat the forces that would dehumanize anyone. We pray for a more just world where all live with dignity.

Prayer

O Lord, with Rosa Parks and Dr. Martin Luther King Jr., empower me to sit for justice and speak boldly against evil. Amen.

The Lord's Prayer: Conclusion

[For the kingdom, the power, and the glory are yours, now and forever.] Amen.

What is this? or *What does this mean?*

That I should be certain that such petitions are acceptable to and heard by our Father in heaven, for he himself commanded us to pray like this and has promised to hear us. "Amen, amen" means "Yes, yes, it is going to come about just like this."

To ponder

Because you are the one in charge, and you have all the power, and the glory is all yours forever—which is just the way we want it!

—Dallas Willard, *The Divine Conspiracy*

Power talk

In many Hispanic Lutheran churches, folks stand up and share how God has answered the prayers of the faithful during the week through the healing of an illness, a life rescued from the ravages of addiction, and so on. As they speak of the power of God over their lives and how their prayers were answered, folks in the congregation chime in, like an echo, with their agreement. All of this proclaims that God knows us and is in control of our lives. God hears and answers our prayers. God has all the power in the world and all glory and honor belong to the Holy One.

Jesus ushers in the reign of God with his life. He gives us a dynamic witness of the power of God over sin, death, and all evil. Because of this, we too have a power story to tell. That is why we say, "Amen!"

Prayer

O Lord, may the power talk of my life honor your holy name. Amen.

March 29

The Sacrament of Holy Baptism

What is baptism?

Baptism is not simply plain water. Instead, it is water used according to God's command and connected with God's word.

What then is this word of God?

Where our Lord Christ says in Matthew 28, "Go therefore and make disciples of all nations, baptizing them in the name of the Father and of the Son and of the Holy Spirit."

To ponder

We are Christians today because Jesus has called us. He has called us through others—through others who themselves were called, and who upon being called also received the commission to go and teach. Therefore, while not forgetting that we have

been commissioned to go and teach, it is also important to remember that we have been called and taught by others.
—Justo L. González, *Jesus Calls*

Word and water united

The baptismal waters flow through more than twenty centuries of the faithful gathering around fancy fonts or on earthen banks doing what Jesus commands. Water varies: different mineral components, sometimes a scarce commodity, other times an overwhelming presence, standing water or flowing, a few drops or full immersion. But the word that is spoken over the waters unites this diversity. God promises to speak and speaks the promise in every time and place. The divine eternal word enters into our particularity, rippling out from that first incarnational splash. In fact, since the human body is about 60 percent water, when the word first became flesh, the word became water! Since Jesus has entered history, word and water are united.

We speak that word on God's behalf to baptismal candidates: you are child of God, hija de Dios, Gotteskind, marked by the cross of Christ forever—the word first spoken to us. The white-gowned day is but the beginning of this pronouncement as we grow together into Jesus-shaped discipleship.

Prayer

Lord, speak to us that you might speak through us of your will to embrace all people. In Jesus' name. Amen.

March 30

The Sacrament of Holy Baptism

What gifts or benefits does baptism grant?

It brings about forgiveness of sins, redeems from death and the devil, and gives eternal salvation to all who believe it, as the words and promise of God declare.

What are these words and promise of God?

Where our Lord Christ says in Mark 16, "The one who believes and is baptized will be saved; but the one who does not believe will be condemned."

To ponder

The Holy Spirit is not only God with us; She is God for us. . . . Filled, inspired, and moved by the Holy Spirit, *evangélicas* [Protestant Latina women] engage life from the perspective of

One who is able to move over chaos, nothingness and death, speaking life into death-bearing situations and being midwives to hope." —Zaida Maldonado Pérez, *Latina Evangélicas*

Overflowing love

Zaida Maldonado Pérez writes about people who work every day for the life promised by the Spirit. They do this through community engagement, the nurturing of families, prayer, and song. All the baptized are called to join in this ministry. God has poured out divine love upon us so that with every step we take, that love sloshes on those around us.

God promises to be with us, bringing life from death, salvation to the hopeless, forgiveness to those who fail. While many may overlook your daily, life-giving work, the Spirit walks with you, tenderly allowing God's grace to spill over your brim, baptizing others in love: the kind word spoken to a stranger in need, diapers changed, mercy extended, the vote cast to feed the hungry, the casserole baked for a grieving soul, the rejected son welcomed by the church family, the lawn mowed, the final prayer spoken. God gathers these up, watching not as judge but as appreciative grandmother, treasuring divine love spilling— like water from the font—on those around us. Baptized by the Spirit, we become midwives of hope to those held by despair.

Prayer

Ever walk with us, Spirit of life, on the journey from brokenness and despair to healing and hope. Amen.

The Sacrament of Holy Baptism

How can water do such great things?

Clearly the water does not do it, but the word of God, which is with and alongside the water, and faith, which trusts this word of God in the water. For without the word of God the water is plain water and not a baptism, but with the word of God it is a baptism, that is, a grace-filled water of life and a "bath of the new birth in the Holy Spirit," as St. Paul says to Titus in chapter 3.

To ponder

God has justified people through Jesus on the cross by an act of grace that destroys the power of sin to control and the power of law to convict. To live out of such grace is to trust by faith in the salvation that comes from God alone. In response to such grace,

people are called to express grace and love to others out of a life of gratitude for what God has done.
—David Rhoads, *The Challenge of Diversity*

Awakening trust

Irene had been hurt badly in her life, and so she was skeptical when Tanya began offering her support. She assumed that this could not be kindness; perhaps she was being set up. But Tanya kept showing up for her over and over again, always without conditions or judgment. Slowly but surely Irene found that Tanya's trustworthiness awakened trust in her. With Tanya's support, she found herself alive and ready to reach out to others. Now she seeks out people who have been abused and compassionately extends a hand. Slowly and persistently she does what it takes to awaken trust.

We have already spoken of water and the word; to this we now add faith, or in everyday language, trust. Trust is not our work, but a gift that God's persistent, steadfast mercy awakens in us. God returns again and again in spite of our resistance to being loved until divine love wins the day. When this happens we find ourselves trusting in God, and the word spoken from eternity finds its home among us. God is as good as God's word, and that word is Jesus.

Prayer

Trustworthy God, awaken trust in us. Amen.

The Sacrament of Holy Baptism

How can water do such great things? (continued)

As St. Paul says to Titus in chapter 3, "through the water of rebirth and renewal by the Holy Spirit. This Spirit he poured out on us richly through Jesus Christ our Savior, so that, having been justified by his grace, we might become heirs according to the hope of eternal life. The saying is sure."

To ponder

If we have learned something from history and from the predicaments we have created, it is that our trust cannot be in humanity but in God, that our help comes not from ourselves but from God. It is when we have learned to trust in God that we can

restore our trust in humanity[,] . . . the humanity rooted in love and compassion . . . deepened and enriched by God's grace.
—C. S. Song, *The Believing Heart*

Meeting us in the mess

The word *justification* rings resoundingly in the Reformation movement. It confesses that God's role is to declare us holy so that we become what we are meant to be. God gives us much responsibility in creation, but God did not consult us before giving us Jesus. Our relationship with God is ever first and foremost God's work and deep desire.

Among the predicaments we have created and the brokenness that bombards us, God comes in Jesus, meeting us in the mess. Embracing the title "friend of sinners," Jesus makes us sinners into friends of God. This is no April Fools' prank. God embraces us in the midst of our errors and makes us heirs of the hope of eternal life. Freed from our own schemes for getting a piece of the inheritance, we settle down into the promise already offered and assured. The death of Christ declares that the inheritance is ours, this day and forever; so also Jesus shares resurrected life with us, this day and forever.

Prayer

Holy God, open our arms to welcome your embrace; open our arms to welcome our neighbors in need as fellow heirs. Amen.

The Sacrament of Holy Baptism

What then is the significance of such a baptism with water?

It signifies that the old person in us with all sins and evil desires is to be drowned and die through daily sorrow for sin and through repentance, and on the other hand that daily a new person is to come forth and rise up to live before God in righteousness and purity forever.

Where is this written?

St. Paul says in Romans 6, "We were buried with Christ through baptism into death, so that, just as Christ was raised from the dead through the glory of the Father, so we too might walk in newness of life."

To ponder

In the valley of the shadow of broken worlds
>   your wings dazzled and light reclaimed its beauty and
>   power....
>   As the love in your eyes sang softly my name
>   the rhythm of your flight resurrected my own.
>   —Aberjhani, *The River of Winged Dreams*

Taking flight

My friend Chris describes a shower he took after a two-week back-packing trip as a deeply spiritual experience. He says, "During my shower, I can remember standing under the water and it seemed that with every drop that hit my head, dirt was replaced by humanity, brokenness was replaced by hope. I went into the shower a tired and worn down shell of myself, and I left the shower as Chris, but a sort of new Chris. It seemed that this shower marked the transition between an experience and a new way of living." Chris went on to connect that shower with the power unleashed in our baptism.

Paul too links our baptism with radical newness. We die to the old self (our failures, betrayals, evil desires, false names, and death) and rise to newness (God's righteousness, fidelity, truthful naming, and resurrected life). The glory of Christ's victory over death shines through us; we take flight daily.

Prayer

Sing softly your love, risen Jesus, that we may rise with you.
Amen.

April 3

How people are to be taught to confess

What is confession?

Confession consists of two parts. One is that we confess our sins. The other is that we receive the absolution, that is, forgiveness, from the pastor as from God himself and by no means doubt but firmly believe that our sins are thereby forgiven before God in heaven.

To ponder

Ministry is first and foremost the ministry of proclamation, the concrete speaking of the word of God, doing the sacramental deed, in the living present. . . . Ministry is absolution—concrete, present-tense, I-to-you declaration in Word and sacrament authorized by the triune God: "I declare unto you the gracious forgiveness of all your sins in the name of the Father, the Son, and the Holy Spirit"... in the here and now, the mystery is made known.

—Gerhard O. Forde, *Theology Is for Proclamation*

Here and now

You, dear reader, have been authorized by God to declare something most wonderful. You stand in for God and declare without ambiguity God's forgiveness of sin to those wearied by the weight of their past. You may or may not be a pastor, but if someone chooses you as their confessor and tells you the things that lie so heavily on their heart, you are called to speak on God's behalf and give them divine forgiveness.

Christians love to talk about forgiveness and how in general we trust that God is a forgiving God. But when someone comes to you and unburdens themselves, the time for generalities has ceased. Look them in the eyes and offer the word that promises them release. "Kelly, I have heard what you have said to me, and you are correct when you say this never should have happened, but I stand before you on Jesus' behalf to say without hesitation and with God's full authority, you are forgiven for Jesus' sake." You have heard a confession that perhaps no one else has ever heard. So the moment is now. Speak!

Prayer

God of grace, fill me with your grace as I speak in Jesus' name. Amen.

April 4

How people are to be taught to confess

Which sins is a person to confess?

Before God one is to acknowledge the guilt for all sins, even those of which we are not aware, as we do in the Lord's Prayer. However, before the pastor we are to confess only those sins of which we are aware and which trouble us.

Which sins are these?

Here reflect on your walk of life in light of the Ten Commandments: whether you are father, mother, son, daughter, master, mistress, servant; whether you have been disobedient, unfaithful, lazy, whether you have harmed anyone by word or deed; whether you have stolen, neglected, wasted, or injured anything.

To ponder

We attempt to disown our difficult stories to appear more whole or more acceptable, but our wholeness—even our wholeheartedness—actually depends on the integration of all of our experiences, including the falls. —Brené Brown, *Rising Strong*

Trusting God's mercy

Every time I visited John he lamented an event from half a century earlier. His baby suffered from a bad cold. He responded as many did back then. A vaporizer created steam through oil and flame. Somehow, the fire spread to the crib, enveloping John's daughter. She was rescued, but bore scars her whole life. So did John's heart. For more than fifty years, John grieved his child's burns. Guilt weighed him down as he second-guessed what he might have done differently. In every visit, John told me this difficult part of his story; my role was to tell him the story of a gracious God who knows what John carries and yet promises, "You are forgiven." John's spirits rose with that promise, although the old accusations did not die easily; perhaps they never died entirely until God spoke to John face-to-face.

God invites us to share all that troubles us so that divine grace may take it on and make us whole.

Prayer

Holy God, you want all that we are, so wholeheartedly we offer ourselves to you, trusting in your mercy, through Jesus Christ. Amen.

The Sacrament of the Altar

What is the Sacrament of the Altar?
It is the true body and blood of our Lord Jesus Christ under the bread and wine, instituted by Christ himself for us Christians to eat and to drink.

To ponder

Our bodies are the most intimate places in which we live out our lives. They are the most intimate places from which we connect ourselves with the world, from which we form relationships. We cannot separate our minds, our spiritual lives, or ourselves from our bodily existence. In that sense, it is really true that we do not have bodies—rather, we are bodies.

—Andrea Bieler and Luise Schottroff, *The Eucharist*

Embodied

Was ist das? What is this? Luther affirmed that when we ask this question of Holy Communion, the answer is simple: it is Jesus, true Jesus. Not cognitively remembering Jesus, not pretending to be with Jesus, not magically Jesus, but Jesus with us. The specifics of "how" were not Luther's concern, as he could embrace mystery. We, on the other hand, have spent countless words and hours debating how Jesus can be truly present.

In such questioning, we might be led to ask about creation: How does God create touchable, edible things, and why are they good? Or we are led to incarnation: How is Jesus truly human and truly God, and why believe in this Embodied One?

Debates will go on. We are thoughtful creatures and such questioning does not distance us from God. Yet we also are bodies: bodies that feel, touch, see, smell, eat, and love. When we come to the table, we are intimately connected with God; we do not just have thoughts about God, we taste God. We don't aspire to reach God, but God is poured out, dribbles down our chins. This is very strange, yet by faith, we are assured that this is true.

Prayer

O God, awaken our bodies to your dwelling within us and with all creation. Amen.

April 6

The Sacrament of the Altar

Where is this written?

The holy evangelists Matthew, Mark, and Luke, and St. Paul write thus:

"In the night in which he was betrayed, our Lord Jesus took bread, and gave thanks, broke it, and gave it to his disciples, saying: Take and eat; this is my body, given for you. Do this for the remembrance of me. Again, after supper, he took the cup, gave thanks, and gave it for all to drink, saying: This cup is the new covenant in my blood, shed for you and for all people for the forgiveness of sin. Do this for the remembrance of me."

To ponder

It is terrible how much has been forgotten, which is why, I

suppose, remembering seems a holy thing.
—Anita Diamant, *The Red Tent*

Re-membering

Breaking and putting back together: remembering does both.
You or someone you know might have had a memory resurface, a
painful memory that sends the mind and body into a downward
spiral. Remembering, as life shows us time and time again, is
not simply a mental exercise of conjuring a picture back into our
minds. No, remembering can break us open in ways we never
could have anticipated.

When we come to the Lord's table, we remember much more
than a night in which Jesus shared a supper and then went to
his death. We are reminded of so much else, especially through a
great prayer that remembers the history of God's remembering
us. In Jesus, we are re-membered: our broken stories, our broken
selves are reassembled into the one who holds us.

Jesus' holiness did not look like holiness; his "otherness"
drove him to eat with the unclean, to heal the forgotten, and to
bless the children. When we remember Jesus, we remember not
only his death, but also his life that drove him to the cross. In
remembering, we see the pieces of his life united in one purpose:
to reveal God's face of mercy and forgiveness.

Prayer

O God, remember what is broken and make me whole again.
Amen.

The Sacrament of the Altar

What is the benefit of such eating and drinking?
The words "given for you" and "shed for you for the forgiveness of sin" show us that forgiveness of sin, life, and salvation are given to us in the sacrament through these words, because where there is forgiveness of sin, there is also life and salvation.

To ponder

Grace makes no conditions and singles out none of us in particular; grace takes us all to its bosom and proclaims general amnesty. See! That which we have chosen is given us, and that which we have refused is, also and at the same time, granted us. Ay, that which we have rejected is poured upon us abundantly.

For mercy and truth have met together, and righteousness and bliss have kissed each other! —Isak Dinesen, "Babette's Feast"

Not nothing, but everything

"Oh, really, you shouldn't have," says the recipient. "It was nothing, really," says the giver. Both statements mask the truth.

When a person gives you a gift you feel you did not deserve, you may say he or she shouldn't have made the effort, but to be honest, you are grateful; you feel blessed by such thoughtfulness. Likewise, when you give a gift, having carefully considered that perfect token to bring joy to another, responding, "It was nothing," devalues your love for them. It shows humility, yes, not to heap praise upon yourself, but your gift was certainly not "nothing."

Question: Can the same conversation happen at the communion table? We hear "given for you," but do we think, "Oh, really, you shouldn't have? O God, you know my failure to love, the anger unleashed, the jealousies festering, the hatred harbored. You really shouldn't have."

Ah, but God revealed in Jesus Christ is the Divine Giver; this is certainly not nothing. It is life. It is a mother's embrace, a father's kiss. God's forgiveness is everything we need to extend gifts of love to one another.

Prayer

O God, in "for you," let us hear your love outpoured, your forgiveness changing everything. Amen.

The Sacrament of the Altar

How can bodily eating and drinking do such a great thing?
Eating and drinking certainly do not do it, but rather the words
that are recorded: "given for you" and "shed for you for the forgiveness of sin." These words, when accompanied by the physical
eating and drinking, are the essential thing in the sacrament, and
whoever believes these very words has what they declare and
state, namely, "forgiveness of sin."

To ponder

We hear your invitation, and heed, O Lord, your call;
your word of consolation is spoken here to all.
It draws us to your loving heart;

it brings to us your blessing, which never will depart.
—Frans Mikael Franzén, "Around You, O Lord Jesus"

Sign and say

Words and actions—we need both. We can say we're sorry,
but if we don't act to right the wrong, words ring empty. We
might have an inkling that the one from whom we've been
estranged intends forgiveness, but we yearn to hear those three
words, "I forgive you."

When we hear endless chatter that seems to be going
nowhere, we give up on words; we dismiss their power to heal.
When rituals are performed haphazardly, we reject the action,
forgetting that in communion and in other rituals—giving a
ring, presenting a diploma, or saluting a flag—we are connected
to truths beyond words.

"In the beginning was the Word, and the Word became flesh."
We come to know about God through scripture, but God is
most clearly shown in Jesus, the living Word. What pure gift:
Jesus' word of forgiveness *and* his life broken and poured out for
you, for the world.

Prayer

O Word Incarnate, give me faith to trust your words and signs
of forgiveness. Amen.

April 9 / Sunday of the Passion

The Sacrament of the Altar

Who, then, receives this sacrament worthily?

Fasting and bodily preparation are in fact a fine external discipline, but a person who has faith in these words, "given for you" and "shed for you for the forgiveness of sin," is really worthy and well prepared. However, a person who does not believe these words or doubts them is unworthy and unprepared, because the words "for you" require truly believing hearts.

To ponder

How we feel about Jesus or how close we feel to God is meaningless next to how God acts upon us. How God indeed enters into our messy lives and loves us through them, whether we want God's help or not. —Nadia Bolz-Weber, *Pastrix*

Unearned treasure

Luther often used the word *treasure* when describing Holy Communion. He also believed that unlike a quest for hidden treasure, this gift comes to us whether we know of it or seek it.

What do you make of unearned treasure in light of the catechism's remarks about worthiness? On the one hand, we don't need to fast. On the other hand, we need truly believing hearts. Does this turn believing into something we need to excel at? How do I know if my heart truly believes today? Last week? Next month? Is "just believing" really good news?

Yes, we come to the table in faith, but faith comes as a gift. We also receive faith by coming to the table, in hearing those words, "for you." We say, "I believe," next to "Help my unbelief" (Mark 9:24). If we had to manufacture perfect faith before receiving, we'd never come. If we had to make sure everything in us was correct before being a spouse, parent, or grandparent, we'd be eternally alone in this life.

We are not worthy; our lives and motives are messy. Yet the treasure box is shining, abounding with good things.

Prayer

Open my heart, O God. In my doubts, awaken faith. I ask in Jesus' name, trusting your loving Spirit. Amen.

The Morning Blessing

In the morning, as soon as you get out of bed, you are to make the sign of the holy cross and say: "God the Father, Son, and Holy Spirit watch over me. Amen."

Then, kneeling or standing, say the Apostles' Creed and the Lord's Prayer. If you wish, you may in addition recite this little prayer as well: "I give thanks to you, heavenly Father, through Jesus Christ your dear Son, that you have protected me through the night from all harm and danger. I ask that you would also protect me today from sin and all evil, so that my life and actions may please you. Into your hands I commend myself: my body, my soul, and all that is mine. Let your holy angel be with me, so that the wicked foe may have no power over me. Amen."

After singing a hymn perhaps (for example, one on the Ten Commandments) or whatever else may serve your devotion, you are to go to your work joyfully.

Morning cross

A quick Internet search will tell you what to do in the morning to ensure your day begins well. You can make to-do lists, eat a nutritious breakfast, meditate, exercise, do a crossword, and the list goes on. If you are a morning person, you might joyfully leap out of bed and get started on any or all. If you are a night owl, you might hit snooze again and wish the world operated on your time clock.

In the Small Catechism, Luther offers a shorter list of morning suggestions: make the sign of the cross, pray, and sing. Is one list better than the other?

What about that sign of the cross? It requires little effort and few words. But like many ritual actions, it works on us over time. Taking less than ten seconds to trace the cross, we remember that our days, routines, and intentions are not really about us. Yes, our plans matter for our work and for our home life. But that brief cross tracing tells us: You are first and foremost a child of God. Like that shoot growing in the morning sun, you arise not by your plans or power, but by God's Spirit.

Prayer

Awaken me, gracious God, to your presence and promise this day and every day. Amen.

April 11

The Evening Blessing

In the evening, when you go to bed, you are to make the sign of the holy cross and say: "God the Father, Son, and Holy Spirit watch over me. Amen."

Then, kneeling or standing, say the Apostles' Creed and the Lord's Prayer. If you wish, you may in addition recite this little prayer as well: "I give thanks to you, heavenly Father, through Jesus Christ your dear Son, that you have graciously protected me today. I ask you to forgive me all my sins, where I have done wrong, and graciously to protect me tonight. Into your hands I commend myself: my body, my soul, and all that is mine. Let your holy angel be with me, so that the wicked foe may have no power over me. Amen."

Then you are to go to sleep quickly and cheerfully.

Plea for protection

"For you alone, O Lord, make me lie down in safety," we pray in Psalm 4. Numerous psalms, Luther's morning and evening prayers, and many other prayers and songs express a yearning for God's protection: O God, keep me safe. Keep my loved ones safe.

When your heart and mind are troubled, sleep does not come quickly or cheerfully. For the child living in fear of her parents, the family facing eviction, or a town threatened by violence or disaster, safety is an urgent, real plea. The wicked foe is not some red character with horns wielding a pitchfork, not some abstract dark force. In especially horrific situations, such as the abuse of a child by a parent, the evil not only is real but comes from the one most expected to love and protect.

If you are fortunate enough to live securely, embraced regularly in loving arms, you still pray for protection because this prayer reminds us that "our body, our soul, and all that is ours" are gifts treasured by God. We pray for ourselves, yes, but at night we also remember those facing danger, praying that God's holy wings shelter them. And once rested, we work tirelessly to protect the vulnerable among us.

Prayer

In your loving arms, O God, grant all your children rest and safety. Amen.

Table Blessing before Meals

The children and the members of the household are to come devoutly to the table, fold their hands, and recite: "The eyes of all wait upon you, O Lord, and you give them their food in due season. You open your hand and satisfy the desire of every living creature."

Then they are to recite the Lord's Prayer and the following prayer: "Lord God, heavenly Father, bless us and these your gifts, which we receive from your bountiful goodness, through Jesus Christ our Lord. Amen."

To ponder

"Repetition is reality, and it is the seriousness of life . . . repetition is the daily bread which satisfies with benediction."

88

Repetition is both as ordinary and necessary as bread, and the very stuff of ecstasy. —Søren Kierkegaard, quoted in Kathleen Norris, *The Quotidian Mysteries*

Just say it

Does that first sentence of Luther's make you chuckle? Perhaps you know of children who come to the table devoutly, hands folded. If so, how lovely and lucky for you! If not, your household pre-dinner narrative might sound something like this: "Come on! We're waiting. Did you wash your hands? Don't touch the grapes yet. Stop kicking your brother. Please put your knees down. Don't eat that—it was on the floor!"

In her book *In the Midst of Chaos: Caring for Children as Spiritual Practice*, Bonnie J. Miller-McLemore describes and encourages "sanctifying the ordinary." Instead of waiting for that serene, devotional moment, we seek out opportunities in the hustle and bustle of life to recognize God's presence.

It might feel like too much work to get everyone seated and ready to pray. Adults and children alike might be fidgety or distracted. Yet the act of taking that moment to say or sing, "Come, Lord Jesus," or "God is great," matters. It is necessary repetition that works its way from our lips into our bones, convincing us that our food and our lives are pure gift.

Prayer

O God, teach us to give thanks in every season. Amen.

April 13 / Maundy Thursday

Table Blessing after Meals

Similarly, after eating they should in the same manner fold their hands and recite devoutly: "Give thanks to the Lord, for the Lord is good, for God's mercy endures forever. God provides food for the cattle and for the young ravens when they cry. God is not impressed by the might of a horse, and has no pleasure in the speed of a runner, but finds pleasure in those who fear the Lord, in those who await God's steadfast love."

Then recite the Lord's Prayer and the following prayer: "We give thanks to you, Lord God our Father, through Jesus Christ our Lord for all your benefits, you who live and reign forever. Amen."

To ponder

Eating with the fullest pleasure . . . is perhaps the profoundest enactment of our connection with the world. We experience and celebrate our dependence and our gratitude, for we are living from mystery, from creatures we did not make and powers we cannot comprehend." —Wendell Berry, *What Are People For?*

Mighty and merciful

It was during dinner. Jesus knelt down, assumed the posture of a servant, and washed feet. Would we do that? Do we even remember to give thanks before leaving the table?

What does gratitude do? At its best, our receiving leads us to sharing, to showing love for one another. Each time we gather to eat, we are reminded that we need nourishment and that a host of people worked to provide it. Yet even when we are full, we are challenged not to display our fullness, but to empty ourselves. How can that food make us both mighty and merciful, both strong and dependent?

This is what Jesus reveals to us, the mystery of a God who, though strong as the mountains, bends low like those cattle in the field and feeds us as young ravens huddled in the nest. We work hard to show our might, but when gratitude creeps in, we discover we are fed best by mercy.

Prayer

Mighty and merciful God, accept our thanks and have patience when we forget our dependence on you. Amen.

April 14 / Good Friday

Luther's Flood Prayer

We give you thanks, O God, for in the beginning your Spirit moved over the waters and by your Word you created the world, calling forth life in which you took delight. Through the waters of the flood you delivered Noah and his family, and through the sea you led your people Israel from slavery into freedom. At the river your Son was baptized by John and anointed by the Holy Spirit. By the baptism of Jesus' death and resurrection you set us free from the power of sin and death and raise us up to live in you.

To ponder

God wants to anticipate now, by the Spirit, a world set right, a world in which the good and joyful gift of justice has flooded creation. —N. T. Wright, *Simply Christian*

Facing the flood

In the darkened theater, my son climbed onto my lap, looking for comfort. The film we watched was not fiction but fact: Hurricane Sandy burst onto the Eastern seaboard, sending waves of destruction through neighborhoods in New York and New Jersey. Lives were swallowed up. He was rightfully frightened. This documentary, "How to Let Go of the World and Love All the Things Climate Can't Change," faces flooding head-on, opening viewers' eyes to communities worldwide challenged by floods and other climate-related destruction.

Scripture assures us that God will never again destroy the world by flood. Can we believe it? Can we respond in hope to this promise, especially those of us who are most vulnerable? Watching the documentary, viewers discover that its creator had a "Holy Spirit" moment. Faced with grim ecological forecasts, he could either be overwhelmed by despair or respond in hope. He chose the latter, finding hope in places we'd least expect. This film was a result, the Spirit working through human creativity.

On this day we dare to call good, we proclaim that death is not the final word. God's people proclaim hope, joined to the one who rose from the waters.

Prayer

Lead us through the waters, O God, and show us your overflowing goodness. Amen.

Luther's Flood Prayer (continued)

Pour out your Holy Spirit, the power of your living Word, that those who are washed in the waters of baptism may be given new life. To you be given honor and praise through Jesus Christ our Lord, in the unity of the Holy Spirit, now and forever.

To ponder

We must put our faith in wings, for after these forty days and forty nights we know that God has tested us and that God is with us. Wings are what we rely on, and they are coming. There is land, and the terrible sustaining waters are sinking away. We have been where no breath can be drawn, but the waters have left us and the air is sweet. —James Dickey, *God's Images*

New life

"I Believe I Can Fly," sings R. Kelley in the 1996 Billboard hit. The 1920s gospel song "I'll Fly Away" carries us up and away to God. Flying equals freedom, or so we are led to believe. Nothing can pin us down. We sail away on currents of air, leaving below all that troubles us. Until we crash.

In baptism, we receive new life. In a sense, we are given new wings. We find freedom in Christ; we are a new creation. But it is God's wings, not our own, that hold us up. We don't escape the hardships of this life—nor should we want to—because God plumbs the depths, too.

Is escape tempting? Just put me on a plane and take me anywhere but here, we might wish. Our baptism, however, holds our feet here on the ground, washes us so we might see more clearly the trials and temptations within and around us. New life? Yes. But a new life tethered to all God would have us be and do in love.

Easter is coming, yet it is already here. We rise with Christ, the one who carries us where we need to go.

Prayer

Free me, O God, to rise in hope and serve in love. Amen.

Notes

March 1: John Irving, *A Prayer for Owen Meany* (HarperCollins, 2012, reprint ed.), 640. **March 2:** Beenish Ahmed, "Learning—and Unlearning—to Be an Ambassador for Islam," *NPR Code Switch: Race and Identity, Remixed,* March 22, 2016. Available at http://www.npr.org/sections/codeswitch/2016/03/22/462380871/learning-and-unlearning-to-be-an-ambassador-for-islam. **March 3:** Alice Walker, "The Welcome Table," in *Listening for God: Contemporary Literature and the Life of Faith,* ed. Paula J. Carlson and Peter S. Hawkins (Augsburg Fortress, 1994), 111. **March 4:** James W. Johnson, "Lift Every Voice and Sing," *Evangelical Lutheran Worship* (Augsburg Fortress, 2006), Hymn 841. **March 5:** Lorna Bradley, *Special Needs Parenting: From Coping to Thriving* (Huff Publishing Associates, 2015), 80. **March 6:** Julia Fordham, "Porcelain," *Porcelain* (Virgin Records US, 1992). **March 7:** Parker J. Palmer, *Healing the Heart of Democracy* (Jossey-Bass, 2011), 90. **March 8:** Anne Lamott, *Bird by Bird* (Random House, 1994), 22. **March 9:** Anne Tyler, "People Who Don't Know the Answers," in *Listening for God Volume 2: Contemporary Literature and the Life of Faith,* ed. Paula J. Carlson and Peter S. Hawkins (Augsburg Fortress, 1996), 41. **March 10:** Neil Simon, "The Seduction," in *The Good Doctor* (Samuel French, Inc., 1974), 437. **March 11:** Theodore Seuss Geisel, *The Lorax* (Random House, 1971). **March 12:** Audre Lorde, *A Burst of Light: Essays by Audre Lorde* (Firebrand Books, 1988). **March 13:** Alice Walker, *The Color Purple* (Harcourt Brace Jovanovich, 1970). **March 14:** Madeleine L'Engle, *Walking on Water: Reflections on Faith and Art* (WaterBrook Press, 1980). **March 15:** Delores Williams, *Sisters in the Wilderness: The Challenge of Womanist God-Talk* (Orbis Books, 1993). **March 16:** Nikki Giovanni, "Love: Is a Human Condition," *The Collected Poetry of Nikki Giovanni: 1968–1998* (Harper Perennial Modern Classics, reprint ed., 2007). **March 17:** Clarissa Pinkola Estés, *Women Who Run with the Wolves: Myths and Stories of the Wild Woman Archetype* (Random House, 1992). **March 18:** Ada Maria Isasi-Diaz, "Mujeristas: A Name of Our Own!!" (*Christian Century,* May 24–31, 1989), 560. **March 19:** Maltbie D. Babcock, "This Is My Father's World," *Evangelical Lutheran Worship* (Augsburg Fortress, 2006), Hymn 824. **March 20:** Argentine traditional, "Holy, Holy, Holy / Santo, Santo, Santo," *Evangelical Lutheran Worship* (Augsburg Fortress, 2006), Hymn 473. **March 21:** Justo L. González, "A Hispanic Creed," in *Mil Voces para Celebrar: Himnario Metodista* (Abingdon Press, 1996), 70. **March 22:** Alicia Vargas, "The Prayer That Jesus Taught Us: A Relational and Communal Life," *The Lutheran* 28, no. 12 (December 2015): 40–41. **March 23:** Sitting Bull, quoted in Mark Diedrich, *The Collected Speeches of Sitting Bull* (Coyote Books, 1998). **March 24:** Ann Voskamp, *One Thousand Gifts: A Dare to Live Fully Right Where You Are* (Zondervan, 2011). **March 25:** Steven McFadden, *The Little Book of Native American Wisdom* (Element King, 1994), 13. **March 26:** C. S. Lewis, *Reflections on the Psalms* (Fontana Books, 1984). **March 27:** Martin Luther King Jr., "I Have a Dream," speech delivered August 28, 1963, Washington, D.C. **March 28:** Dallas Willard, *The Divine Conspiracy: Rediscovering Our Hidden Life in God* (Harper, 1998), 269. **March 29:** Justo L. González, *Jesus Calls* (Abingdon Press, 2004), 93. **March 30:** Loida I. Mertell-Otero, Zaida Maldonado Pérez, and Elizabeth Conde-Frazier, *Latina Evangélicas: A Theological Survey from the Margins* (Cascade Books, 2013), 16. **March 31:** David Rhoads, *The Challenge of Diversity: The Witness of Paul and the Gospels* (Fortress Press, 1996), 23. **April 1:** C. S. Song, *The Believing Heart: An Invitation to Story Theology* (Fortress Press, 1999), 239. **April 2:** Aberjhani, *The River of Winged Dreams* (Bright Skylark Literary Productions and Lulu, 2010), 60. **April 3:** Gerhard O. Forde, *Theology Is for Proclamation* (Fortress Press, 1990), 179. **April 4:** Brené Brown, *Rising Strong: The Reckoning. The Rumble. The Revolution* (Spiegel & Grau, 2015), 43. **April 5:** Andrea Bieler and Luise Schottrof, *The Eucharist: Bodies, Bread, and Resurrection* (Fortress Press, 2007), 133. **April 6:** Anita Diamant, *The Red Tent* (St. Martin's Press, 1997), 3. **April 7:** Isak Dinesen, "Babette's Feast," *Anecdotes of Destiny* (Random House, 1958). **April 8:** Frans Mikael Franzén, "Around You, O Lord Jesus," *Evangelical Lutheran Worship* (Augsburg Fortress, 2006), Hymn 468. **April 9:** Nadia Bolz-Weber, *Pastrix: The Cranky, Beautiful Faith of a Sinner and Saint* (Jericho Books, 2013), 176–77. **April 12:** Søren Kierkegaard, quoted in Kathleen Norris, *The Quotidian Mysteries* (Paulist Press, 1998), 28; and Bonnie J. Miller-McLemore, *In the Midst of Chaos: Caring for Children as Spiritual Practice* (Jossey-Bass, 2006). **April 13:** Wendell Berry, "The Pleasures of Eating," in *What Are People For?* (North Point Press, 1990), 152. **April 14:** N. T. Wright, *Simply Christian: Why Christianity Makes Sense* (HarperCollins, 2006), 136. **April 15:** James Dickey, *God's Images: A New Vision* (Harper & Row, 1984).